Photographic Memories

Francis Frith's
Derbyshire

Revised edition of original work by

Clive Hardy

FRITH
BOOK CO

First published in the United Kingdom in 1998
by WBC Ltd

Revised paperback edition published in the United Kingdom in 2000 by
Frith Book Company Ltd
ISBN 1-85937-196-5

Hardback Reprinted in 2000
ISBN 1-85937-283-x

British Library Cataloguing in Publication Data

Francis Frith's Derbyshire
Clive Hardy

Frith Book Company Ltd
Frith's Barn, Teffont,
Salisbury, Wiltshire SP3 5QP
Tel: +44 (0) 1722 716 376
Email: info@frithbook.co.uk
www.frithbook.co.uk

Printed and bound in Great Britain

AS WITH ANY HISTORICAL DATABASE THE FRITH ARCHIVE IS CONSTANTLY BEING CORRECTED AND IMPROVED
AND THE PUBLISHERS WOULD WELCOME INFORMATION ON OMISSIONS OR INACCURACIES

Contents

Francis Frith: *Victorian Pioneer*

FRANCIS FRITH, Victorian founder of the world-famous photographic archive, was a complex and multitudinous man. A devout Quaker and a highly successful Victorian businessman, he was both philosophic by nature and pioneering in outlook.

By 1855 Francis Frith had already established a wholesale grocery business in Liverpool, and sold it for the astonishing sum of £200,000, which is the equivalent today of over £15,000,000. Now a multi-millionaire, he was able to indulge his passion for travel. As a child he had pored over travel books written by early explorers, and his fancy and imagination had been stirred by family holidays to the sublime mountain regions of Wales and Scotland. 'What a land of spirit-stirring and enriching scenes and places!' he had written. He was to return to these scenes of grandeur in later years to 'recapture the thousands of vivid and tender memories', but with a different purpose. Now in his thirties, and captivated by the new science of photography, Frith set out on a series of pioneering journeys to the Nile regions that occupied him from 1856 until 1860.

Intrigue and Adventure

He took with him on his travels a specially-designed wicker carriage that acted as both dark-room and sleeping chamber. These far-flung journeys were packed with intrigue and adventure. In his life story, written when he was sixty-three, Frith tells of being held captive by bandits, and of fighting 'an awful midnight battle to the very point of surrender with a deadly pack of hungry, wild dogs'. Sporting flowing Arab costume, Frith arrived at Akaba by camel seventy years before Lawrence, where he encountered 'desert princes and rival sheikhs, blazing with jewel-hilted swords'.

During these extraordinary adventures he was assiduously exploring the desert regions bordering the Nile and patiently recording the antiquities and peoples with his camera. He was the first photographer to venture beyond the sixth cataract. Africa was still the mysterious 'Dark Continent', and Stanley and Livingstone's historic meeting was a decade into the future. The conditions for picture taking confound belief. He laboured for hours in his wicker dark-room in the sweltering heat of the desert, while the volatile chemicals fizzed dangerously in their trays. Often he was forced to work in remote tombs and caves where conditions were cooler. Back in London he exhibited his photographs and was 'rapturously cheered' by members of the Royal Society. His reputation as a photographer was made overnight. An eminent modern historian has likened their impact on the population of the time to that on our own generation of the first photographs taken on the surface of the moon.

Venture of a Life-Time

Characteristically, Frith quickly spotted the opportunity to create a new business as a specialist publisher of photographs. He lived in an era of immense and sometimes violent change. For the poor in the early part of Victoria's reign work was a drudge and the hours long, and people had precious little free time to enjoy themselves. Most had no transport other than a cart or gig at their disposal, and had not travelled far beyond the

boundaries of their own town or village. However, by the 1870s, the railways had threaded their way across the country, and Bank Holidays and half-day Saturdays had been made obligatory by Act of Parliament. All of a sudden the ordinary working man and his family were able to enjoy days out and see a little more of the world.

With characteristic business acumen, Francis Frith foresaw that these new tourists would enjoy having souvenirs to commemorate their days out. In 1860 he married Mary Ann Rosling and set out with the intention of photographing every city, town and village in Britain. For the next thirty years he travelled the country by train and by pony and trap, producing fine photographs of seaside resorts and beauty spots that were keenly bought by millions of Victorians. These prints were painstakingly pasted into family albums and pored over during the dark nights of winter, rekindling precious memories of summer excursions.

The Rise of Frith & Co

Frith's studio was soon supplying retail shops all over the country. To meet the demand he gathered about him a small team of photographers, and published the work of independent artist-photographers of the calibre of Roger Fenton and Francis Bedford. In order to gain some understanding of the scale of Frith's business one only has to look at the catalogue issued by Frith & Co in 1886: it runs to some 670 pages, listing not only many thousands of views of the British Isles but also many photographs of most European countries, and China, Japan, the USA and

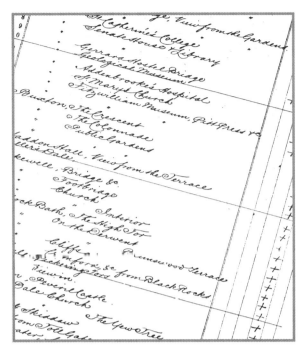

Canada – note the sample page shown above from the hand-written *Frith & Co* ledgers detailing pictures taken. By 1890 Frith had created the greatest specialist photographic publishing company in the world, with over 2,000 outlets – more than the combined number that Boots and WH Smith have today! The picture on the right shows the *Frith & Co* display board at Ingleton in the Yorkshire Dales. Beautifully constructed with mahogany frame and gilt inserts, it could display up to a dozen local scenes.

Postcard Bonanza

The ever-popular holiday postcard we know today took many years to develop. In 1870 the Post Office issued the first plain cards, with a pre-printed stamp on one face. In 1894 they allowed other publishers' cards to be sent through the mail with an attached adhesive halfpenny stamp. Demand grew rapidly, and in 1895 a new size of postcard was permitted called the court card, but there was little room for illustration. In 1899, a year after Frith's death, a new card measuring 5.5 x 3.5 inches became the standard format, but it was not until 1902 that the divided back came into being, with address and message on one face and a full-size illustration on the other. *Frith & Co* were in the vanguard of postcard development, and Frith's sons Eustace and Cyril continued their father's monumental task, expanding the number of views offered to the public and recording more and more places in Britain, as the coasts and countryside were opened up to mass travel.

Francis Frith died in 1898 at his villa in Cannes, his great project still growing. The archive he created continued in business for another seventy years. By 1970 it contained over a third of a million pictures of 7,000 cities, towns and villages. The massive photographic record Frith has left to us stands as a living monument to a special and very remarkable man.

Frith's Archive: *A Unique Legacy*

FRANCIS FRITH'S legacy to us today is of immense significance and value, for the magnificent archive of evocative photographs he created provides a unique record of change in 7,000 cities, towns and villages throughout Britain over a century and more. Frith and his fellow studio photographers revisited locations many times down the years to update their views, compiling for us an enthralling and colourful pageant of British life and character.

We tend to think of Frith's sepia views of Britain as nostalgic, for most of us use them to conjure up memories of places in our own lives with which we have family associations. It often makes us forget that to Francis Frith they were records of daily life as it was actually being lived in the cities, towns and villages of his day. The Victorian age was one of great and often bewildering change for ordinary people, and though

the pictures evoke an impression of slower times, life was as busy and hectic as it is today.

We are fortunate that Frith was a photographer of the people, dedicated to recording the minutiae of everyday life. For it is this sheer wealth of visual data, the painstaking chronicle of changes in dress, transport, street layouts, buildings, housing, engineering and landscape that captivates us so much today. His remarkable images offer us a powerful link with the past and with the lives of our ancestors.

Today's Technology

Computers have now made it possible for Frith's many thousands of images to be accessed almost instantly. In the Frith archive today, each photograph is carefully 'digitised' then stored on a CD Rom. Frith archivists can locate a single photograph amongst thousands within seconds. Views can be catalogued and sorted under a variety of categories of place and content to the immediate benefit of researchers.

Inexpensive reference prints can be created for them at the touch of a mouse button, and a wide range of books and other printed materials assembled and published for a wider, more general readership - in the next twelve months over a hundred Frith local history titles will be published! The day-to-day workings of the archive are very different from how they were in Francis Frith's time: imagine the herculean task of sorting through eleven tons of glass negatives as Frith had to do to locate a particular

See Frith at www. frithbook.co.uk

sequence of pictures! Yet the archive still prides itself on maintaining the same high standards of excellence laid down by Francis Frith, including the painstaking cataloguing and indexing of every view.

It is curious to reflect on how the internet now allows researchers in America and elsewhere greater instant access to the archive than Frith himself ever enjoyed. Many thousands of individual views can be called up on screen within seconds on one of the Frith internet sites, enabling people living continents away to revisit the streets of their ancestral home town, or view places in Britain where they have enjoyed holidays. Many overseas researchers welcome the chance to view special theme selections, such as transport, sports, costume and ancient monuments.

We are certain that Francis Frith would have heartily approved of these modern developments in imaging techniques, for he himself was always working at the very limits of Victorian photographic technology.

The Value of the Archive Today

Because of the benefits brought by the computer, Frith's images are increasingly studied by social historians, by researchers into genealogy and ancestory, by architects, town planners, and by teachers and schoolchildren involved in local history projects.

In addition, the archive offers every one of us an opportunity to examine the places where we and our families have lived and worked down the years. Highly successful in Frith's own era, the archive is now, a century and more on, entering a new phase of popularity.

The Past in Tune with the Future

Historians consider the Francis Frith Collection to be of prime national importance. It is the only archive of its kind remaining in private ownership and has been valued at a million pounds. However, this figure is now rapidly increasing as digital technology enables more and more people around the world to enjoy its benefits.

Francis Frith's archive is now housed in an historic timber barn in the beautiful village of Teffont in Wiltshire. Its founder would not recognize the archive office as it is today. In place of the many thousands of dusty boxes containing glass plate negatives and an all-pervading odour of photographic chemicals, there are now ranks of computer screens. He would be amazed to watch his images travelling round the world at unimaginable speeds through network and internet lines.

The archive's future is both bright and exciting. Francis Frith, with his unshakeable belief in making photographs available to the greatest number of people, would undoubtedly approve of what is being done today with his lifetime's work. His photographs, depicting our shared past, are now bringing pleasure and enlightenment to millions around the world a century and more after his death.

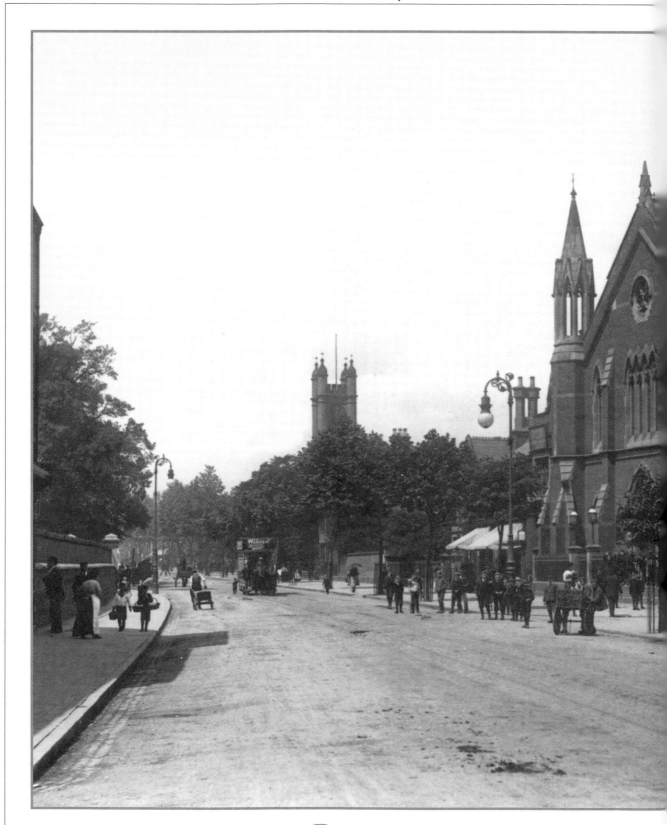

Around Derby

Derby

This county town has a history going back to at least the Roman times, who then occupied the area now known as Little Chester. Derby was later one of the five towns of the Danelaw, along with Lincoln, Leicester, Stamford and Nottingham. It fell to the Saxons in AD 941. In 1745 Derby was the southern most point reached by Charles Edward Stuart during his invasion of England. Had Charles not turned back for Scotland, the whole course of British history would have been different. Derby's modern growth was due to it being chosen as the headquarters and main workshops for the Midland Railway. Good rail connections soon led to other industries opening for business, and the population rocketed to over 114,000 by 1901.

Derby, London Road 1896 37781A
A horse tram trundles along London Road in the general direction of Alvaston, but it could turn off and head for the Midland Station. In the background is the tower of Holy Trinity Church, a private development built under the name of St George's. The developer went bust and the church was eventually sold and renamed.

▼ Derby, St Peter's Church 1896 37786

The inhabitants of St Peter's parish used to take part in the local Shrovetide football matches against St Werburgh's parish. There were hundreds of players on each side, rules were few and far between, and the playing area was the streets of the town. The game was finally banned in 1846, and today, only the town of Ashbourne carries on the tradition.

▼ Derby, Victoria Street 1896 37778

The corner is dominated by the Athenaeum and the Royal Hotel, built in 1839 at a cost of £20,000.

▲ Derby, Irongate and All Saints Church 1896 37780

The town centre was partially redeveloped during the nineteenth century, both St Peter's Street and Irongate were widened, Markeaton Brook was culverted over, the Shambles in the Market Place were demolished, and a new road bridge was built over the Derwent. This is Irongate in 1896.

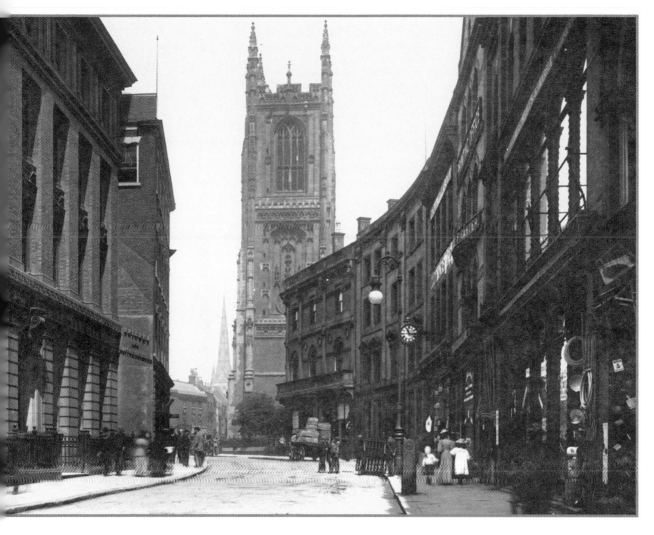

◄ **Derby, Town Hall 1896**
37776A
This view was taken three years after gaslamps had been replaced by electric street lighting. The horse trams started running in the 1880s and survived until 1904, when they were replaced by electric trams. The electric trams lasted only until 1934 when they too were replaced, this time by trolleybuses.

**Derby, Corn Market
1896** 37779
Looking down the Corn
Market to the Market
Place. On the left-hand
side of the street stand
a couple of cabs, which
were an expensive way
to travel. In 1906 the
cab fare from the
Midland Station to the
Royal Hotel was 1s 6d.

Derby, All Saints Church 1896 37783

Derby, On the Derwent 1896 37789
In the picture is the tower of St Mary's and the spire of St Alkmund's. Partially hidden by the trees on the right, is the chapel of St Mary's-on-the-Bridge.

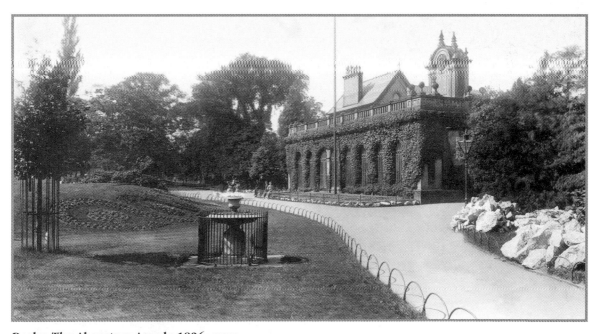

Derby, The Aboretum Arcade 1896 37792
When the Arboretum opened in September 1840 it was the first public park in the country. The land, donated by Joseph Strutt, was planted with every variety of tree and shrub capable of withstanding the climate. Such was the interest in the Arboretum that the Midland Railway were able to fill excursion trains to Derby. This picture taken in 1896 shows the main entrance at Arboretum Street.

Derby, St Aulkmund's Church 1896 37784
Built in 1846 at a cost of £9,000 on the site of an earlier church, St Alkmund's is named after the son of the deposed Northumbrian King Alured. Alkmund was martyred in AD 800 on the orders of King Eardulph, and is said to have eventually been buried at Derby.

Derby, The Aboretum 1896 37790
The ornamental fountain and fishpond situated at the centre of the Arboretum. The irregular paths and undulating mounds made the park appear much bigger than it actually was.

Allestree, Markeaton Park, c1960 A200027
Markeaton Park is many times bigger than the Arboretum. Over the years this park has been developed to become one of the city's main areas for recreation and leisure.

◀ **Ashbourne 1955**
A66045
A general view of
Ashbourne taken in
1955. The practice
tower at the fire station
can be seen on the right,
beyond which, is the
memorial gardens and
cattle market.

Ashbourne & Dovedale

Ashbourne

Once a small market town of around 4,000 people, it is now a fashionable place to live for those able to escape from Derby. Ashbourne has an interesting history; King Charles prayed in St Oswald's Church after the Battle of Naseby, Dr Johnson was a regular visitor to the Mansion House, and during the Napoleonic Wars some 300 French prisoners were billeted here. It was the French prisoners who gave the town its local delicacy, gingerbread, with its own special flavour.

▲ **Ashbourne, The Market Place 1957** A66018
The buildings remain very much the same, though some of the businesses are long gone. The porticoed Town Hall is in the middle of the block.

Ashbourne, St Oswald's, South West 1896 37875 ▶
St Oswald's Church was consecrated in 1241, and it was here that King Charles attended a service after the Battle of Naseby in 1645. The church is renowned for its remarkable series of monuments to the Cockayne family, and the famous Carrara marble figure of five-year-old Penelope Boothby who died in 1791.

◄ **Dovedale, Dove Holes
& Captains Rock 1894**
34258
The twin caverns of
Dove Holes, form one of
the chief features of the
dale. Across the river
stands the Captain's
Rock and Looker's Hill.
In 1894 the latter was
part of Stanshope Hall
Farm, which had been
owned by the
Beardmore family for
several generations.

Dovedale

In Victorian times it was considered that the best way to see Dovedale was to catch a train to Alsop-en-le-Dale station and then walk. The Dove was famous for trout fishing, the best stretch of water being between the Stepping Stones and the wooden bridge.

▲ **Dovedale, Doveholes 1894** 34257
The twin caverns known as Dove Holes, as they looked in 1894. The larger cavern was home to a variety of lichens, and liverwort grew in abundance. Visitors to the larger cavern were encouraged to test the echo by shouting an alleged Dovedale shepherds' call of 'Whup! whup! whup! whup! wo-o-o wo-o fo-o'! Try it.

**Dovedale, Reynards ▶
Cave 1914** 67604
Settling down to a picnic in front of Reynard's Cave. The natural arch through which the cave can be seen, probably has no equal in the UK.

Dovedale, The Stepping Stones 1914 67609
A little further, on a footbridge led to the Isaac Walton Hotel, where rooms cost from 3s 6d and lunch or dinner from 2s 6d.

Dovedale, Reynards ▶
Cave 1914 67603
Looking down from
Reynard's Cave to where
our picnicking friends in
the previous picture had
been. Note the rope,
which was a necessary aid
for those wishing to
explore the cavern.

▼ **Dovedale, Thorpe Cloud**
1894 34263
An 1894 picture of Thorpe
Cloud. Alsop-en-le-Dale
station is 3 miles and 1,408
yds away, Thorpe Cloud
station a mere 1 mile and 384
yds. The donkeys were
available for hire.

◄ **Duffield, Town Street c1950** D1593090
The view is still pretty much the same today. By the side of Tamworth Street is an old stone bridge over the River Ecclesbourne, which was made from stone salvaged from the castle ruins.

Around & About on the Road to Buxton

Duffield

Duffield once boasted one of the greatest fortresses in England. It belonged to the Earl of Derby along with the castles at Tutbury and Oakham. In 1263 the earl was defeated by Henry III, and though his possessions were ordered forfeit to the crown, the earl was pardoned on condition that if he rebelled again he would be disinherited. He did and he was. Duffield Castle was demolished and much of its stone used in local buildings.

◀ **Duffield, From the Bank c1950** D1593093
Here the River Derwent swings round in a long lazy S-bend; Duffield is in the distance.

◀ **Duffield, The Bridge over the River Derwent c1950**
D1593092

◄ **Belper, The River and Mill c1955** B437015
Though Jebediah Strutt was a considerate employer who even provided a cottage hospital for his workers, he does not appear to have had any qualms about employing young children in his mills to clean the machinery.

Belper

Belper was originally called Beaurepaire, after its pleasant location on the banks of the River Derwent. The earliest industry appears to have been nail making, the first recorded instance being in 1313, but this eventually died out during the nineteenth century. Belper's expansion was due to Jebediah Strutt, who opened textile mills and built homes for his workers.

◀ **Belper, Bridge Street c1955** B437019
On the right is the Lion Hotel where a room in 1906 cost 3s a night and dinner 2s 6d. In the distance is one of the mills which towered above the rooftops.

◀ **Belper, From Crich Lane c1955** B437031

**Ambergate, View from ▶
Canal Bank, c1955**

A203017

Ambergate once boasted a triangular railway station, serving routes to Derby, Sheffield and Manchester. The station still survives, but it has been reduced to the status of an unstaffed halt, and the lines connecting the former route to Manchester with those to Sheffield have been removed.

Ambergate

Ambergate was chosen by George Stephenson as the site for a series of limekilns, the stone coming from Cliff Quarry, Crich. The quarry closed in 1957 and the limekilns followed suit in 1965.

◀ **Ambergate, Matlock Road c1955** A203023A
A train pulls out of Ambergate in the direction of Manchester. The road on the right leads to Ripley, on the left is the Hurt Arms.

◄ **Cromford,
Willersley Castle
c1955** C193023
Willersley Castle at
Cromford was built by
Sir Richard Arkwright for
his own use, but he died
before its completion.

Cromford

Cromford was chosen by Richard Arkwright in 1772, as the site for the first textile factory in the world to be equipped with water-powered cotton-spinning machinery. The mill made use of the water pumped out of one of the local mines; it was delivered over a cast-iron aqueduct which still stands to this day. Arkwright had no problems with transporting raw materials and finished goods, as the Cromford Canal basin was across the road from the mill.

◀ **Cromford, Lea Hurst 1892** 31296
Lea Hurst, near Cromford, was once the home of Florence Nightingale. Her family owned a textile mill at Lea which they eventually sold to John Smedley. Nearby is Lea Gardens, which was established over fifty years ago in a worked-out quarry, and has over 500 species of Rhododendron's growing there.

◀ **Cromford, Willersley Castle c1955** C193012
Willersley Castle later became a Methodist guest house.

Cromford, The Village 1892 31290A
The large building in the foreground is the Greyhound Inn, built in 1778 for the benefit of visitors to Arkwright's mill. Arkwright also built cottages, a school and a church, for his workers.

Cromford, The Bridge 1886 18578
The fifteenth century Cromford Bridge as it looked in 1886. The bridge stands near the entrance to Willersley Castle. An unusual feature is that on one side of the bridge the arches are pointed, whilst on the other side they are rounded.

Cromford, The Bridge 1892 31293
Cromford Bridge from the rounded arch side. Among the trees is an early eighteenth century fishing temple.

◄ Wirksworth c1960

W351007

As well as lead-mining, there were also a number of limestone quarries in the vicinity, including Bowne & Shaw's, Hopton Wood, Wirksworth Lime & Stone and Killer's Middleton Quarry. Wirksworth was used by George Eliot as background material for her novel Adam Bede.

Wirksworth

For centuries, Wirksworth was the most important centre in the county for lead-mining; the Moot Hall houses an oblong bronze dish dating from 1513, which is still the standard measure for a pig of lead. This is also where Britain's oldest industrial court, the Barmoot Court, sits on matters relating to the conduct of the lead-mining industry. To this day, members of the court smoke clay pipes after their meal.

◄ **Black Rocks 1892** 31294
Near the summit of the steep hill on the road to Wirksworth, stand the Black Rocks. This picture dates from 1892, the rocks already a tourist attraction for many years.

◄ **Wirksworth, St Mary's Church, 1960** W351004
St Mary's stands in the middle of a circular churchyard, and might be the area occupied in Anglo-Saxon times. In 1820 a stone coffin lid, dating from around AD 800 was found under the floor of the church.

Via Gellia

With a name like Via Gellia, it would be easy to assume that the place had some connection with the Roman occupation. Alas, this is not the case. The road was in fact built in 1791-2 by Philip Gell of Hopton Hall, for the transportation of ore from his lead mines to a smelter at Cromford.

Via Gellia, Tufa Cottage 1892 31298
Tufa Cottage still stands, but it would be hard today to recreate this tranquil scene as this road is now the busy A5012, a favourite haunt of heavy lorries.

**Via Gellia, The Pig
of Lead public house
1892** 31300
Near here is the old
Carrington Viyella
factory; the Viyella trade
name being a play on
Via Gellia.

◄ **Matlock Bath,
The Mill Weir 1892**
31289
On the left bank Sir
Richard Arkwright built a
mill in 1793. In 1898 the
mill was sold to the
English Sewing Cotton
Co., who expanded the
factory to around double
its previous size. The
limestone crags
overlooking the far bank
are a favourite with
climbers, and some of
the routes are more
difficult and dangerous
than they look.

Matlock Bath

Once upon a time, Derbyshire was one of the main centres for lead mining, and around 100,000 mine shafts have been located and recorded. Matlock Bath was no exception, and there were several mines here, the earliest going back to the Roman occupation. Just a few miles away, the Mill Close Mine at Darley Dale became the biggest lead mine in the country. Mill Close survived until 1939-40, when problems with flooding made it uneconomic to continue working. The warm springs at Matlock Bath began to attract public attention as early as 1698, but is was not until the 1850s that the area began to rival Buxton.

◄ **Matlock Bath, Steel 1892** 31274
Since this picture was taken, the Royal Museum which opened around 1829, has been demolished. The buildings on the left and the petrifying well are still there.

◄ **Matlock Bath, New Bath Hotel, c1955** M47016
Visitors could bath in the tepid spring waters at the New Bath Hotel, the Royal Hotel and the Fountain Baths. In 1906 rooms at the New Bath cost from 4s 6d a day, the Royal being somewhat cheaper at 3s 6d.

▼ **Matlock Bath, Grand Pavilion, c1955** M47041

The Grand Pavilion, once used for concerts, now houses the Mining Museum run by the Peak District Mines Historical Society. One of the features of the museum are the simulated mine shafts and assages which can be explored.

▼ **Matlock Bath, The Fish Pond, c1955** M47005

The ornamental fishpond and fountain is situated to one side of the Grand Pavilion. The constant temperature in the pond allows it to be stocked with fish other than goldfish. This picture was taken in 1955; the strings of coloured lights could mean that the town is getting ready for its illuminations.

▲ **Matlock Bank, Footbridge 1886** 18611

In the foreground is the footbridge leading to Lovers' Walks. In the distance is the bridge leading to Matlock Bath Station. In keeping with the surrounding countryside, the station was built in the Swiss Chalet style.

◄ **Matlock Bath, Lovers' Walks 1892** 31284
It is along here that most of the displays for the illuminations are sited. The illuminations were so popular that the railway used to run special trains and offer special day return tickets.

▼ **Matlock Bath, Lovers' Walks 1892** 31284A

▼ **Matlock Bath, Jubilee Bridge, c1955** M47064
Boating down the river on a sunny afternoon in 1955. The Jubilee Bridge replaced the earlier footbridge. Boating is in fact, confined to a short stretch of the river, due to there being a weir in the direction of Cromford.

▲ **Matlock Bath, Derwent Terrace 1892** 31276
Though the buildings remain pretty much the same, this road is now the extremely busy A6, and there is usually a string of cars parked all the way down the left-hand side of the highway.

◄ **Matlock Bath, North Parade and the Derwent c1955** M47038
On the far hill is Riber Castle built by John Smedley, the hydropathic Godfather of Matlock. It was Smedley who got the hydropathic ball rolling in Matlock, when he opened a small establishment at Matlock Bank in 1850.

**Matlock Bath,
Derwent Terrace
1892** 31279
Looking in the direction
of the Grand Pavilion.
The Promenade has
been reduced in width
over the years to allow
for road widening. Part
of the gardens in the
picture still remain; it is
where the War
Memorial is
now situated.

Matlock Bath, North Parade from The Royal Hotel 1892

31272

The picture is taken from the bridge leading to the railway station. The view is recognisable today, though the street lights have been replaced with modern standards, and some of the shop fronts have been remodelled.

◄ **Matlock Bath,
High Tor 1892** 31285
The entrance to the Tor
is upstream from the
railway station. In 1906
the admission price was
3d each, but the view
from the top was
considered well worth
the money.

◀ **Matlock Bath, From the Pavilion c1900** M47301
This shows Derbyshire scenery at its best, with Matlock Bath straggling the narrow valley through which the Derwent flows.

Matlock Bath, ▶
High Tor 1892 31288B
High Tor a dramatic limestone crag rising to a height of 380 ft dominates Matlock Bath. The picture was taken in 1892.

◀ **Matlock, The Dale c1955** M273302
High Tor is on the left, and the Derwent is all but obscured by trees, with the A6 snaking its way alongside. To the right of the road are the Heights of Abraham, who were given their name by an officer who had served with General Wolfe at Quebec.

◀ **Matlock, Bank Road c1950** M273004
In this picture we get some idea of just how steep this road is. The tramway was on a steeper incline than the famous cable cars of San Fransisco; the fare being 2d to go up hill and 1d to come down.

Matlock

Matlock owes its development as a spa town to John Smedley, who in 1850 opened a small hydropathic establishment with rooms for six guests. Eventually, there were around thirty hydros, including Chesterfield House, Matlock House and the Rockside. The town's other industries included a couple of limestone quarries and textile mills.

◀ **Matlock, Bank Road from Crown Square c1955**
M273005
It was along here that many of the Hydros were established, and from 1893 to 1927 the steep hill was served by a cable operated tramway.

◀ **Matlock, Hall Leys Pleasure Gardens c1955** M273002
The small pavilion with the clock on top is the old tram shelter that used to be at the Crown Square terminus. Riber Castle was used as a school for about twenty years before being abandoned in 1950. In 1962 it became a zoological garden for British and European wildlife.

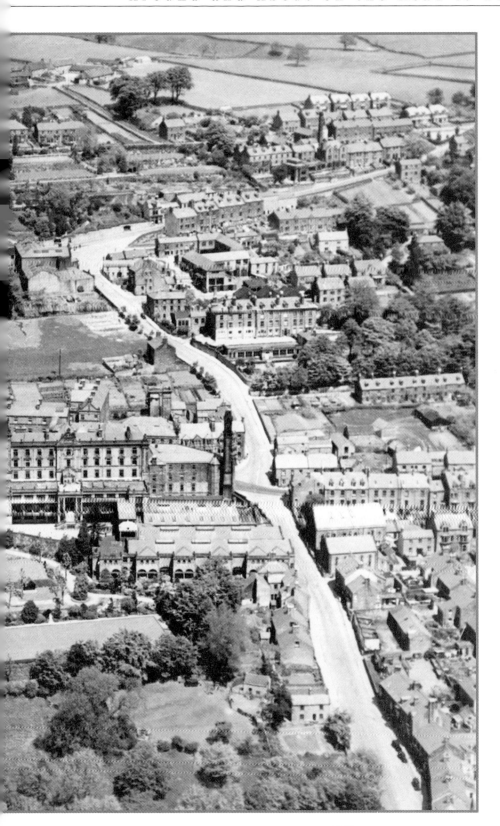

Matlock, c1955
M273301
The large building in the centre of the picture is John Smedley's hydro, which was built in 1853 and extended as business expanded. The castellated part dates from the late 1860s, and there were further additions in 1885.

◀ **Matlock,**
The Boating Lake,
Hali Leys Gardens
c1955 M273062

◄ **Matlock, The Winter Gardens, Smedley's Hydro c1955** M273038 The Winter Gardens at Smedley's hydro in 1955, the year it finally closed. The buildings were taken over as offices for Derbyshire County Council.

▼ **Matlock, Darley Dale, between Matlock and Rowsley c1955** M273053 In the far distance is Riber Castle. In the churchyard is a yew tree, reputed to be the oldest tree in Britain.

◄ **Matlock, Darley Dale c1955** M273056 Darley Dale Caravan Park, 1955 when such things were still a rarity away from the coast.

◄ **Matlock, Darley Dale
The Pool c1955**
M273049
'Come in twenty-three,
your time's up.' In the
Frith Collection records
this is called the Darley
Dale Pleasure Gardens.

◀ **Matlock, Darley Dale, Caravan Park c1955**
M273042
A close-up of the caravans, which today look a bit like garden sheds on wheels. You can bet there isn't a television, fridge, microwave or a barbecue between the lot of them.

▼ **Matlock, The Pleasure Gardens c1955**
M273046
The Pleasure Gardens were directly opposite the caravan site, and for 1955 it is pleasantly laid out with plenty of places to sit and lots of things for the kids to do.

◀ **Chatsworth House 1886** 18643
Chatsworth, the magnificent stately home of the Dukes of Devonshire, seen here in 1886. Built between 1687 and 1706 with the north wing added in 1820, Chatsworth remains a veritable treasure house.

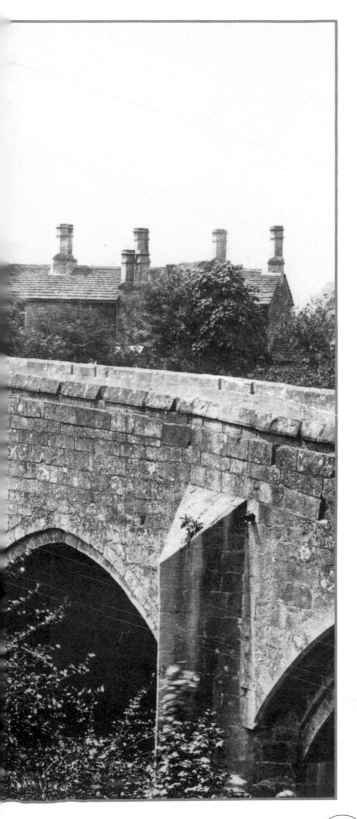

Rowsley

The village of Rowsley at the head of Darley Dale, was for a few months the northern terminus of the grandly titled Manchester, Buxton, Matlock & Midlands Junction Railway. Opened in 1848, the railway was jointly leased by the LNWR and the Midland. When the Midland, who operated the line, commenced their extension from Rowsley to Buxton, a realignment of the route meant that a new passenger station had to be built, the old one being relegated to a goods depot.

Rowsley, Bridge & Peacock Inn, 1904 5216
The old bridge over the river. Beyond, lies the village and the Peacock Hotel. The hotel was originally built in 1625 as a house for a certain John Stevenson. It became an inn in 1828.

Rowsley, The Peacock Inn 1886 18617
The inn, which belonged to the Duke of Rutland, got its name from the peacock badge of the Manners family. Being situated at the confluence of the Wye and the Derwent, the Peacock was a popular place with anglers. In 1906 a room cost 4s a night.

Haddon Hall

Haddon Hall was the seat of the Vernon family for over 400 years, but passed to the Dukes of Rutland on the marriage of Dorothy Vernon to Sir John Manners. The Hall ceased to be a residence in 1703, but continued to be maintained with the result that it is one of the finest examples of a sixteenth century residence in the country.

Haddon Hall, Entrance Tower 1886 18630
Visitors wait patiently for the Hall to open, in this picture taken in 1886. The earliest parts of the Hall are the north-east tower and part of the chapel, both of which are late-Norman. The south façade and the terraced gardens are sixteenth century.

Bakewell

Famous for its Bakewell puddings which have been made to the same recipe since 1859, the town also has a warm spring which comes to the surface at a constant temperature of 15oC. Bakewell never caught on as a spa town, being overshadowed by Buxton and Matlock. A tourist guidebook for 1906 describes the baths as 'unimportant'.

Bakewell, Rutland Square 1914 67616
This is where Jane Austen stayed while writing Pride and Prejudice. To the right is All Saints Parish Church with its octagonal spire, Norman doorway and a Saxon cross in the churchyard.

◀ **Ashford in the Water, Holy Trinity Church c1955** A324020
The parish church of Holy Trinity was rebuilt during the nineteenth century, but managed to retain some of its Norman features. Inside the church hang four paper garlands, which hark back to the days when such things were carried at funerals. In the churchyard are some interesting memorials, including one to a young man who died on a visit to the World's Fair in the USA.

Ashford in the Water

Ashford was once a key crossing point over the River Wye, protected by a fort. Around the eleventh century, lead-smelting was carried out, and at a later date quarrying for marble was undertaken nearby.

◄ **Ashford in the Water, The Day's Work Done, c1955** A324001
There are three bridges over the Wye, the oldest being the very narrow Sheepwash Bridge. Ashford was an important crossing place for packhorse trains and horse-drawn wagons.

◄ **Ashford in the Water, Top Pump 1955**
A324017
Until the A6 bypassed the village, Ashford was on the road from Derby to Manchester.

◄ **Monsal Dale, The Valley from Monsal Head 1955**

M223006

The railway is on the left-hand side of the valley, the view is in the direction of Monsal Dale station, which was built to serve Cressbrook Mill and the Monsal Dale Spar Mine.

Monsal Dale

Monsal Dale was once described as 'The Arcadia of Derbyshire' and has been popular with walkers for decades. The area is rich with spectacular scenery augmented by the meandering River Wye.

◄ **Monsal Dale, The Viaduct 1914** 67588
A Manchester-bound passenger train has just emerged from Headstone Tunnel and onto the curved viaduct over the River Wye at Monsal Dale. The picture was taken in 1914.

◄ **Monsal Dale, The Monsal Head Hotel c1955** M223004
The two previous pictures were taken from here, the cameraman on each occasion standing where the benches are, but with his back to the hotel.

◄ **Millers Dale,
The Village 1914** 67598
There has been a corn
mill here since 1767, and
nearby is Litton Mill,
which earned itself a
dark reputation for its
use of child labour
during the
nineteenth century.

Miller's Dale

Miller's Dale was the interchange station for rail passengers to and from Buxton, and the Miller's Dale Lime Co. were an important source of mineral traffic.

▲ **Ashwood Dale,
on the outskirts of Buxton c1876** 8822
The road twists and turns through the narrow valley of well-worn limestone rock. On the right, obscured by trees is the Buxton to Millers Dale line of the Midland Railway.

**Ashwood Dale, ▶
Lovers Leap c1862** 1473
One mile out of Buxton on the Bakewell Road, is Sherwood Dell and the cliff called Lover's Leap.

◄ **Buxton, Ashwood Park cascade, looking toward the town centre 1923**
74131
This is at Lower Buxton, the road to Bakewell is on the left. The viaduct still carries the railway, only these days it is freight, only serving Dowlow and Hindlow quarries.

Buxton

There are only two places in the country that have hot springs bubbling to the surface. Bath is one, Buxton is the other, and both were known to the Romans. After the collapse of Roman rule, the springs probably fell into disuse for a time, as the Church considered bathing to be immoral; certain monastic orders and the Knights Templer did not wash at all. By Tudor times however, the efficacious effects of the waters led to the development of Buxton as a spa town.

◄ **Buxton, New Baths 1902**
48186
This view was taken a couple of years or so after the removal of the original colonnading. The bathchairs were available for hire, with the bathchair man pushing the passenger from one treatment to another.

◄ **Buxton, Devonshire Hospital 1896** 37855
Built in 1789 as The Great Stables, the first floor became a hospital in 1857, though the ground floor remained in use as a stables until 1877. Between 1879 and 1881 the building was converted for use as a hospital, which included the addition of what was the largest unsupported domed roof in the world.

◄ **Buxton, The Pavilion Interior, 1890** 24734
The interior of the Pavilion looking towards the Concert Hall. Designed by Robert Rippon Duke, the Concert Hall with seating for up to 1,000 people, was opened in 1876.

◄ **Buxton, From the Slopes, 1932** 85213
The Devonshire Hospital with its unique domed roof is in the background, as is the Palace Hotel. To the left of the Crescent are the Natural Baths and the St Ann's Hotel; to the right are the Hot Baths. In front of the Crescent, which was built between 1780 and 1790 is the Pump Room.

▼ **Buxton, The Pavilion Gardens, 1886** 18657
The entrance to the Central Hall as seen from the gardens in 1886. The building was designed by Edward Milner, who had worked for Joseph Paxton on the project to resite the Crystal Palace at Sydenham, following the Great Exhibition of 1851. The gardens were designed by Edward's son, Henry.

◄ **Buxton, The Tennis Courts in the Gardens, 1886** 18659
From 1884 the Buxton Improvements Committee staged an annual tournament which included the All-England Ladies' Doubles Championship. The last tournament to be held at Buxton was in 1954.

**Buxton, Broadwalk
1914** 67575
Broadwalk, with the
entrance to the gardens
on the left. Originally
known as Cavendish
Terrace, development
began in the 1860s,
and Broadwalk soon
became a fashionable
place to live or
take rooms.

Goyt's Valley 1914
67584
The Goyt was one of
the excursions available
to tourists visiting
Buxton. Here, several
groups have stopped in
order to take lunch
which was supplied by
the hotels.

◀ **Goyt's Valley
and Stepping Stones
1914** 67587
The bridge was on an
old packhorse route.
This part of the Goyt is
now under Errwood
Reservoir, but the bridge
was dismantled and
rebuilt up stream.

◄ **Goyt's Valley 1894**
34246
The rugged and spectacular landscape of the Goyt Valley. The view is in the direction of where the reservoir was to be built in the 1960s.

▼ **Buxton,
The Cat & Fiddle 1894** 34244
The Cat & Fiddle on the Buxton to Macclesfield Road, was and still is the highest public house in England, with a full licence. This picture was taken in 1894, when the pub was a popular watering hole for visitors on a trip out from Buxton. For the energetic there was a combined excursion to Axe Edge.

◄ **Buxton,
The Cat & Fiddle 1914**
67581
Horse-drawn vehicles have given way to the internal combustion engine but the pub remains much the same. The building dates from the 1830s, and has been enlarged since these pictures were taken. It has been known for the pub to be cut off for days during heavy snowfalls.

North West to Chesterfield

Ilkeston

Ilkeston is said to have got its name from a pirate named Elcha, who around AD 600 had nothing better to do than sail up the Humber on a raid. Elcha and his men are said to have settled in east Derbyshire. Here Elcha built a defensive earthwork called a tun, hence Elkeston.

Ilkeston, Bath Street c1955 137040
The road by today's standards is positively devoid of traffic, as private car ownership was still something of a novelty. Even if a family had a car, it was often the case that the wife would still be expected to walk or take public transport to the shops.

Ripley

There were coal mines to the north, south and east of Ripley, such as Denby Drury Low and Denby Old Hall. At Butterley was the long established ironworks, whose products included the supporting pillars for the roof of St Pancras Station. Mining still survives in the area, though much of it is now opencast and the ironworks is still in business.

Ripley, Grosvenor Road, c1955 R299020

◀ **Ripley, Church Street c1955** R299018
The road to the left leads to Butterley, and on the right is the A610 to Nottingham. As with other towns of this size, the high street stores were present. On the left we have Woolworths and a small branch of Burtons.

Ripley, The Market Place c1965 R299042
The large building to the right is the Town Hall. The area has been redeveloped, though it is still recognisable.

Ripley, Butterley ▶ Liftpark c1965 R299062
The one and only Butterley Liftpark, 1965. This strange looking contraption stood near Butterley Ironworks, and was an interesting attempt to find a way of parking a reasonable number of cars in a limited space.

◀ **Ripley, Butterley Reservoir, c1955** R299009
Butterley Reservoir has been popular with anglers for many years. The track of the Midland Railway Centre runs alongside.

**Ripley, New Street
1965** R299045
Taken in the days when
you had to have
separate aerials if you
wanted to watch either
BBC or ITV television
programmes.

◄ **Alfreston,
From Wingfield Road
c1960** A199027

Alfreton

Once a typical east Derbyshire mining town. Benjamin Outram, born near Alfreton in 1764, became a skilled engineer and gained a reputation as a tramway builder. One of his well known tramways was the 5-mile line linking Denby Drury Low Colliery with the Little Eaton Branch of the Derby Canal.

◄ **Alfreton, High Street c1950** A199016
On the left is the Tudor style Odeon Cinema, whilst across the road we have the usual high street chain stores of Woolworths and Burtons.

◄ **Alfreton, The Hall, c1960** A199005
Alfreton Hall was built in 1730, with additional wings being added during the nineteenth century. At the entrance to the Hall grounds stands St Martin's Church.

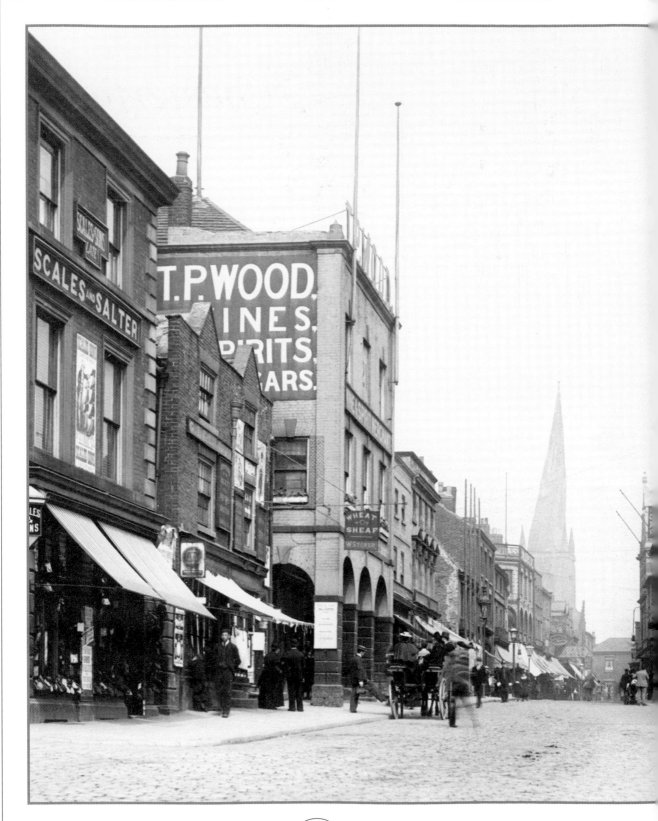

Chesterfield

The second largest town in the county. Chesterfield's history goes back to Roman times, though its modern development was due to the fact that it lay in the midst of a busy coal-mining district, which in turn attracted other industry including, Staveley and Sheepbridge ironworks and Markham & Co. Despite this, Chesterfield is mainly famous for the crooked spire of St Mary and All Saints. Although the spire looks as if it will collapse at any second, it has a very low centre of gravity and is therefore quite safe.

Chesterfield, High Street 1896 37801
A view along High Street, with the Market Place on the right and Scales & Salter's boot and shoe shop on the left. The building next to Salters was demolished and replaced by a grand three-storey affair housing T. Spencer & Co.

Chesterfield, High Street 1902

48884

Further along the High Street is the Post Office and the Angel Hotel. In the distance we have a good view of the twist in the spire of St Mary's and All Saints Church. The lead-covered timber spire which is 228 ft high, leans out of true some 6 ft to the south and over 4 ft to the west.

◄ **Chesterfield, Hotel
Portland 1902** 48898
The Portland Hotel,
where a room would
cost around 3s 6d a
night and a good lunch
could be had for
half-a-crown.

Chesterfield, The Market Hall 1902

48883

The Market Hall dominates this picture of the Market Place. In those days markets were only held on Saturdays, the Market Place packed with traders stalls. In recent years the market has been extended to three days a week.

Chesterfield, Stephenson Place 1914 67563

Named after George Stephenson, who was the engineer responsible for routing the North Midland Railway through Chesterfield. Stephenson spent the last years of his life living at Tapton House and is buried in Holy Trinity Church.

Old Whittington, The Revolution House, c1955 0129007

The Revolution House at Old Whittington was where, in 1688, the Earl of Devonshire and others plotted the overthrow of King James II, to replace him with the protestant William of Orange.

Chesterfield, Stephenson Memorial Hall 1902 48890
The Memorial Hall contained an engineering museum and a library. Today it is also the home of the Pomegranate
Theatre.

Chesterfield, Queen's Park, 1902 48894
The park offered the town's population of over 27,000 somewhere to go, away from the soot and the grime. In the 1960s it was upgraded, with the addition of a sports stadium and running track.

◄ **Eckington, Renishaw Hall c1955**
E226007
Once the home of the talented Sitwell family, Renishaw is now a country park open to the general public.

Bolsover

Five miles east of Chesterfield is the small mining town of Bolsover, whose main employers were the local colliery and the coalite works. On a wooded hill above the town stands Bolsover Castle. There was a fortress here in Norman times, but the present buildings date from 1613.

◀ **Bolsover, The Castle, 1902** 48905
The present castle was built by Sir Charles Cavendish, father of the first Duke of Newcastle. Though it looks like a fortress, Bolsover was built as a magnificent stately home; it is thought Sir Charles was trying to recreate a medieval atmosphere. The castle has a superb indoor riding school, and rooms with names such as the Heaven Room and the Star Chamber. King Charles I entertained here, to a performance of Ben Jonson's masque Love's Welcome.

◀ **Eckington, The village c1955** E226003
The drab brickwork of Eckington village. Eckington's inhabitants found work in nearby collieries, at Renishaw or Staveley Ironworks.

**◄ Chapel-en-le-Frith
Market Street, c1960**

C400004

This was the main shopping street of the town, and business was good enough to support four butchers shops, a bakery, greengrocers, chemists, clothing and shoe shops and several newsagents.

West to East
Chapel-en-le-Frith

The town's history goes back many centuries, and it is likely that it started as a settlement for men working in the Peak Forest. What is unusual is the fact that the parish church is dedicated to St Thomas Beckett, and was founded just a few years after his murder.

◄ **Chapel-en-le Frith, Market Place, c1960** C400003
Chapel-en-le-Frith market place is 776 ft above sea level, and comes complete with a seventeenth century cross and a set of stocks. The tower of the parish church can be seen in the background. The present church was erected in the eighteenth century, replacing the original early fourteenth century building.

◄ **Chapel-en-le-Frith, The Stocks, c1960**
C400002
The stocks were capable of holding two felons side-by-side. People were normally sentenced to serve a number of consecutive market days in the stocks (usually two or three). For some crimes this was the total punishment, but for others there might also be a term of imprisonment.

◄ **Castleton, Speedwell Cavern, Winnats Pass 1909** 61785
The spectacular Winnats Pass and the entrance to the Speedwell Cavern. Speedwell was driven into the hillside in an unsuccessful search for lead-ore during the eighteenth century. Speedwell's unique feature is its subterranean canal, approximately 750 yds long at the end of which is the cavern.

Castleton

Castleton was once an important centre for lead mining, so important in fact, that William the Conqueror gave land to William Peveril to build a castle. It was around the foot of the castles steep northern slope that the village grew, protected by a ditch and earthwork. The lead mining continued for centuries; the other mineral to be mined being Blue John stone which is found nowhere else in the world.

◄ **Castleton, Market Place, 1909** 61776
Peveril Castle can be seen on the hill 260 ft above the village. The original entrance to the castle was from the south-west, across a drawbridge over a rocky ditch. The castle was in Scottish hands for a number of years, but was returned to the crown following an agreement signed at Peveril, by Henry II and Malcolm of Scotland. Henry then set about rebuilding the place, including the addition of a keep.

◄ **Castleton, How Lane, 1919** 69169
Here they offered livery accommodation for horse-drawn vehicles and parking for motor cars. Rooms at local hotels cost 2s a night during the season with dinner costing 2s 6d.

◄ **Bradwell, The Village, 1919** 69174
The village of Bradwell at the north end of the Edale valley, 1919. Once a thriving lead-mining community, the main source of work today is the local cement works. One of the old lead-mines is still in use as access to Bagshawe Cavern. The local miners used to make their own hard hats for wearing underground. They were known as Bradwell Beavers.

Hope

Hope, two miles east of Castleton, is situated at the crossroads of two ancient highways, and the Romans are known to have had a military installation nearby. The village church dates from the fourteenth century, and is noted for its crude gargoyles; there is also the remains of a ninth century cross in the churchyard.

◀ Hope,
The Village Smithy 1932 85261
In the background is the Old Hall Hotel, which sold Truswell's celebrated ales.

◀ **Ladybower, The Dam and Win Hill c1955**
L294006
Ladybower is one of three reservoirs, the others being the Howden and the Derwent. The dams are famous as the training area used by 617 Squadron RAF, prior to carrying out their raid on the German dams which supplied the Ruhr. Every year the last surviving Lancaster Bomber makes a low level pass over the area on the anniversary of the raid.

◄ **Hathersage,
The Village 1902**
48915
This is a photograph of
the main road to
Sheffield as it looked in
1902. The George Hotel
was completely rebuilt,
and the building to its
right was eventually
redeveloped for William
& Glyns Bank.

Hathersage

Around eight miles north of Bakewell stands the hillside town of Hathersage. Legend has it that Robin Hood's friend, Little John, was born here and lies buried in St Michael's churchyard. Charlotte Bronte stayed at the vicarage in 1845, the rector Henry Nussey, proposed to her but she declined him. Charlotte's novel Jane Eyre is set around the area, Hathersage appearing in the book under the name of Morton. Local industry centred on the manufacture of pins and needles. It is also said that Little John was a nailer prior to joining Robin Hood.

◄ **Hathersage, The Village 1902** 48914
Apart from the lamp outside the Ordnance Arms, the cottages opposite had no effective street lighting. Also note that there is a complete absence of telegraph poles.

◄ **Hathersage, The Village 1902** 48917
On the right is the Ordnance Arms Hotel, and the small building just beyond is the bank. The bank was later replaced by a rather grand three-storey affair which later became the National Westminster.

◄ **Middleton Vale,
Looking West 1896**

37821

It was from Lover's Leap around 1760 that a young woman threw herself. Miraculously, she survived the fall receiving only slight injuries. In 1851, William Adam writing in Gem of The Peak retold the girl's story but concluded that her attempted suicide 'wasn't serious.'

Eyam

The village of Eyam found itself a place in the history books thanks to the sacrifice made by its inhabitants during the Great Plague of 1665-6. When the plague reached Eyam in a consignment of cloth from London, the villagers, encouraged by their vicar William Mompesson, decided to isolate themselves from the outside world in an attempt to contain the outbreak. Though the disease abated during the winter months, it returned with avengance in 1666. In all 257 villagers died.

◀ **Eyam Village, North End 1896** 37812
Some of the plague victims were buried outside the churchyard, possibly in an attempt to stop infection within the community. The seven members of the Hancock family were interred in a walled enclosure near to Riley House Farm. An interesting statistic is that during the twentieth century, plague has killed 18 million people worldwide.

▲ **Middleton Entrance and Lovers Leap** 37820
Situated on what is now the very busy A623 Chapel-en-le-Frith to Chesterfield road, Stoney Middleton is a picture of peace and tranquillity in this photograph taken in 1896. In the middle is the Lover's Leap Cafe.

◀ **Froggatt Edge, From Egam Road, 1896** 37827
The villages of Calver and Froggatt have long been a jumping off point for walkers visiting Froggatt Edge. The rocky outcrop of the Edge can be seen in the distance in this picture dating from 1896. In 1803-04, Sir Richard Arkwright opened a cotton mill at Calver providing the locals with an alternative source of employment. The mill was used in the filming of the television series Colditz.

Baslow

The ancient narrow bridge over the Derwent at Baslow, 1883. Baslow village is divided into three parts; Over End, Nether End and Bridge End, though most visitors seem to congregate around the pubs, green and village hall at Nether End.

Baslow, Thatch End, c1955 B484020 ▶
Thatched cottages are fairly rare in this part of Derbyshire. These are at Thatch End, Baslow, 1955.

Baslow, Hydropathic Establishment c1884 16582
Baslow was on the hydropathic bandwagon, along with just about everywhere else in Derbyshire. In 1906 rooms cost from 3s 6d a day, dinner 5s, pensions (room, meals and attendance) were available from 10s 6d a day. A coach and four still made the daily trip to Sheffield, the fare being 1s 6d each way.

Index

Frith Book Co Titles

Frith Book Company publish over 100 new titles each year. For latest catalogue please contact Frith Book Co.

Town Books 96pp, 100 photos. County and Themed Books 128pp, 150 photos (unless specified) All titles hardback laminated case and jacket except those indicated pb (paperback)

Around Bakewell	1-85937-113-2	£12.99	Isle of Man	1-85937-065-9	£14.99
Around Barnstaple	1-85937-084-5	£12.99	Isle of Wight	1-85937-114-0	£14.99
Around Bath	1-85937-097-7	£12.99	Around Leicester	1-85937-073-x	£12.99
Around Blackpool	1-85937-049-7	£12.99	Around Lincoln	1-85937-111-6	£12.99
Around Bognor Regis	1-85937-055-1	£12.99	Around Liverpool	1-85937-051-9	£12.99
Around Bournemouth	1-85937-067-5	£12.99	Around Maidstone	1-85937-056-X	£12.99
Around Bristol	1-85937-050-0	£12.99	North Yorkshire	1-85937-048-9	£14.99
British Life A Century Ago			Northumberland and Tyne & Wear		
	1-85937-103-5	£17.99		1-85937-072-1	£14.99
Around Cambridge	1-85937-092-6	£12.99	Around Nottingham	1-85937-060-8	£12.99
Cambridgeshire	1-85937-086-1	£14.99	Around Oxford	1-85937-096-9	£12.99
Cheshire	1-85937-045-4	£14.99	Oxfordshire	1-85937-076-4	£14.99
Around Chester	1-85937-090-X	£12.99	Around Penzance	1-85937-069-1	£12.99
Around Chesterfield	1-85937-071-3	£12.99	Around Plymouth	1-85937-119-1	£12.99
Around Chichester	1-85937-089-6	£12.99	Around Reading	1-85937-087-X	£12.99
Cornwall	1-85937-054-3	£14.99	Around St Ives	1-85937-068-3	£12.99
Cotswolds	1-85937-099-3	£14.99	Around Salisbury	1-85937-091-8	£12.99
Cumbria	1-85937-101-9	£14.99	Around Scarborough	1-85937-104-3	£12.99
Around Derby	1-85937-046-2	£12.99	Scottish Castles	1-85937-077-2	£14.99
Devon	1-85937-052-7	£14.99	Around Sevenoaks and Tonbridge		
Dorset	1-85937-075-6	£14.99		1-85937-057-8	£12.99
Dorset Coast	1-85937-062-4	£14.99	Sheffield and S Yorkshire		
Down the Thames	1-85937-121-3	£14.99		1-85937-070-5	£14.99
Around Dublin	1-85937-058-6	£12.99	Around Southport	1-85937-106-x	£12.99
East Anglia	1-85937-059-4	£14.99	Around Shrewsbury	1-85937-110-8	£12.99
Around Eastbourne	1-85937-061-6	£12.99	Shropshire	1-85937-083-7	£14.99
English Castles	1-85937-078-0	£14.99	South Devon Coast	1-85937-107-8	£14.99
Essex	1-85937-082-9	£14.99	Staffordshire	1-85937-047-0 (96pp)	£12.99
Around Exeter	1-85937-126-4	£12.99	Around Stratford upon Avon		
Around Falmouth	1-85937-066-7	£12.99		1-85937-098-5	£12.99
Around Great Yarmouth			Suffolk	1-85937-074-8	£14.99
	1-85937-085-3	£12.99	Surrey	1-85937-081-0	£14.99
Greater Manchester	1-85937-108-6	£14.99	Around Torbay	1-85937-063-2	£12.99
Hampshire	1-85937-064-0	£14.99	Welsh Castles	1-85937-120-5	£14.99
Around Harrogate	1-85937-112-4	£12.99	West Midlands	1-85937-109-4	£14.99
Hertfordshire	1-85937-079-9	£14.99	Wiltshire	1-85937-053-5	£14.99

Canals and Waterways	1-85937-129-9	£17.99	Apr
Around Guildford	1-85937-117-5	£12.99	Apr
Around Horsham	1-85937-127-2	£12.99	Apr
Around Ipswich	1-85937-133-7	£12.99	Apr
Ireland (pb)	1-85937-181-7	£9.99	Apr
London (pb)	1-85937-183-3	£9.99	Apr
New Forest	1-85937-128-0	£14.99	Apr
Around Newark	1-85937-105-1	£12.99	Apr
Around Newquay	1-85937-140-x	£12.99	Apr
Scotland (pb)	1-85937-182-5	£9.99	Apr
Around Southampton	1-85937-088-8	£12.99	Apr
Sussex (pb)	1-85937-184-1	£9.99	Apr
Around Winchester	1-85937-139-6	£12.99	Apr
Around Belfast	1-85937-094-2	£12.99	May
Colchester (pb)	1-85937-188-4	£8.99	May
Dartmoor	1-85937-145-0	£14.99	May
Exmoor	1-85937-132-9	£14.99	May
Leicestershire (pb)	1-85937-185-x	£9.99	May
Lincolnshire	1-85937-135-3	£14.99	May
North Devon Coast	1-85937-146-9	£14.99	May
Nottinghamshire (pb)	1-85937-187-6	£9.99	May
Peak District	1-85937-100-0	£14.99	May
Redhill to Reigate	1-85937-137-x	£12.99	May
Around Truro	1-85937-147-7	£12.99	May
Yorkshire (pb)	1-85937-186-8	£9.99	May
Berkshire (pb)	1-85937-191-4	£9.99	Jun
Brighton (pb)	1-85937-192-2	£8.99	Jun
Churches of Berkshire	1-85937-170-1	£17.99	Jun
Churches of Dorset	1-85937-172-8	£17.99	Jun
Derbyshire (pb)	1-85937-196-5	£9.99	Jun
East Sussex	1-85937-130-2	£14.99	Jun
Edinburgh (pb)	1-85937-193-0	£8.99	Jun
Norwich (pb)	1-85937-194-9	£8.99	Jun
South Devon Living Memories			
	1-85937-168-x	£14.99	Jun

Stone Circles & Ancient Monuments			
	1-85937-143-4	£17.99	Jun
Victorian & Edwardian Kent			
	1-85937-149-3	£14.99	Jun
Warwickshire (pb)	1-85937-203-1	£9.99	Jun
Buckinghamshire (pb)	1-85937-200-7	£9.99	Jul
Kent (pb)	1-85937-189-2	£9.99	Jul
Kent Living Memories	1-85937-125-6	£14.99	Jul
Victorian & Edwardian Yorkshire			
	1-85937-154-x	£14.99	Jul
West Sussex	1-85937-148-5	£14.99	Jul
Cornish Coast	1-85937-163-9	£14.99	Aug
County Durham	1-85937-123-x	£14.99	Aug
Croydon Living Memories			
	1-85937-162-0	£12.99	Aug
Dorsert Living Memories			
	1-85937-210-4	£14.99	Aug
Down the Severn	1-85937-118-3	£14.99	Aug
Folkstone	1-85937-124-8	£12.99	Aug
Glasgow (pb)	1-85937-190-6	£8.99	Aug
Gloucestershire	1-85937-102-7	£14.99	Aug
Herefordshire	1-85937-174-4	£14.99	Aug
Lancashire (pb)	1-85937-197-3	£9.99	Aug
Manchester (pb)	1-85937-198-1	£8.99	Aug
Margate, Ramsgate & Broadstairs			
	1-85937-116-7	£12.99	Aug
North London	1-85937-206-6	£14.99	Aug
Picturesque Harbours	1-85937-208-2	£17.99	Aug
Somerset	1-85937-153-1	£14.99	Aug
Teeside	1-85937-211-2	£14.99	Aug
Worcestershire	1-85937-152-3	£14.99	Aug
Victorian & Edwardian Maritime Album			
	1-85937-144-2	£17.99	Aug
Yorkshire Living Memories			
	1-85937-166-3	£14.99	Aug

Available from your local bookshop or from the publisher

FRITH PRODUCTS & SERVICES

Francis Frith would doubtless be pleased to know that the pioneering publishing venture he started in 1860 still continues today. More than a hundred and thirty years later, The Francis Frith Collection continues in the same innovative tradition and is now one of the foremost publishers of vintage photographs in the world. Some of the current activities include:

Interior Decoration

Today Frith's photographs can be seen framed and as giant wall murals in thousands of pubs, restaurants, hotels, banks, retail stores and other public buildings throughout the country. In every case they enhance the unique local atmosphere of the places they depict and provide reminders of gentler days in an increasingly busy and frenetic world.

Product Promotions

Frith products have been used by many major companies to promote the sales of their own products or to reinforce their own history and heritage. Brands include Hovis bread, Courage beers, Scots Porage Oats, Colman's mustard, Cadbury's foods, Mellow Birds coffee, Dunhill pipe tobacco, Guinness, and Bulmer's Cider.

Genealogy and Family History

As the interest in family history and roots grows world-wide, more and more people are turning to Frith's photographs of Great Britain for images of the towns, villages and streets where their ancestors lived; and, of course, photographs of the churches and chapels where their ancestors were christened, married and buried are an essential part of every genealogy tree and family album.

A series of easy-to-use CD Roms is planned for publication, and an increasing number of Frith photographs will be able to be viewed on specialist genealogy sites. A growing range of Frith books will be available on CD.

Frith Products

All Frith photographs are available Framed or just as Mounted Prints, and can be ordered from the address below. From time to time other products - Address Books, Calendars, Table Mats, etc - are available.

The Internet

Already thousands of Frith photographs can be viewed and purchased on the internet. By the end of the year 2000 some 60,000 Frith photographs will be available on the internet. The number of sites is constantly expanding, each focussing on different products and services from the Collection.

Some of the sites are listed below.

www.townpages.co.uk
www.icollector.com
www.barclaysquare.co.uk
www.cornwall-online.co.uk

For more detailed information on Frith companies and products, look at these sites:

www.francisfrith.co.uk
www.frithbook.co.uk
www.francisfrith.com

See the complete list of Frith Books at:

www.frithbook.co.uk

This web site is regularly updated with the latest list of publications from the Frith Book Company Ltd. If you wish to buy books relating to another part of the country that your local bookshop does not stock, you may purchase on-line.

For further information, trade, or author enquiries please contact us at the address below:
The Francis Frith Collection, Frith's Barn, Teffont, Salisbury, Wiltshire, England SP3 5QP.
Tel: +44 (0)1722 716 376 Fax: +44 (0)1722 716 881 Email: uksales@francisfrith.com

To receive your FREE Mounted Print

Cut out this Voucher and return it with your remittance for £1.50 to cover postage and handling. Choose any photograph included in this book. Your SEPIA print will be A4 in size, and mounted in a cream mount with burgundy rule lines, overall size 14 x 11 inches.

Order additional Mounted Prints at HALF PRICE (only £7.49 each*)

If there are further pictures you would like to order, possibly as gifts for friends and family, acquire them at half price (no additional postage and handling required).

Have your Mounted Prints framed*

For an additional £14.95 per print you can have your chosen Mounted Print framed in an elegant polished wood and gilt moulding, overall size 16 x 13 inches (no additional postage and handling required).

---

* IMPORTANT!
These special prices are only available if ordered using the original voucher on this page (no copies permitted) and at the same time as your free Mounted Print, for delivery to the same address

---

Voucher for FREE and Reduced Price Frith Prints

Picture no.	Page number	Qty	Mounted @ £7.49	Framed + £14.95	Total Cost
		1	**Free of charge***	£	£
			£7.49	£	£
			£7.49	£	£
			£7.49	£	£
			£7.49	£	£
			£7.49	£	£

Please allow 28 days for delivery   * Post & handling | £1.50

Book Title ....   **Total Order Cost** | £

Please do not photocopy this voucher. Only the original is valid, so please cut it out and return it to us.

I enclose a cheque / postal order for £ . . . . made payable to 'The Francis Frith Collection' OR please debit my Mastercard / Visa / Switch / Amex card

Number . . . .

Expires . . . . Signature . . . .

Name Mr/Mrs/Ms . . . .

Address . . . .

. . . .

. . . .

. . . . Postcode . . . .

Daytime Tel No . . . .   Valid to 31/12/01

Frith Collectors' Guild

From time to time we publish a magazine of news and stories about Frith photographs and further special offers of Frith products. If you would like 12 months FREE membership, please return this form.

Send completed forms to:
The Francis Frith Collection, Frith's Barn, Teffont, Salisbury, Wiltshire SP3 5QP

The Francis Frith Collectors' Guild

Please enrol me as a member for 12 months free of charge.

Name Mr/Mrs/Ms . . . .

Address . . . .

. . . .

. . . . Postcode . . . .

Free Print - see overleaf